Contents

How your model fits together

1

To replace the body parts in your model, first lay the assembled skeleton inside the back section of the plastic body. Remove the top of the skull, insert the brain, and replace the skull top.

2

Next, place the heart between the two lungs. Then insert this unit into the back rib cage. The prongs on the back of the lungs fit into the four holes at the front of the backbone.

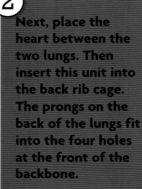

3

Take the urinary system and insert it below the lungs. Make sure that the side showing the kidneys faces outward. Attach it to the backbone so that it rests within the pelvis.

4

Hold the liver round-side up. Then attach the stomach by fitting the short prong into the hole on the underside of the liver. Attach both to the urinary system, directly beneath the lungs.

5

Now place the intestines in the space between the liver/stomach unit and the pelvis. The prong on the back of the intestines fits into the hole halfway down the urinary system.

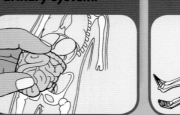

6

Next, position the ribs so that they cover the heart and lungs like a cage.

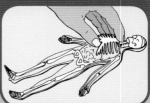

7

Finally, replace the front section of the plastic body, and close the two halves securely.

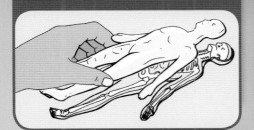

8

To make your model stand upright, place it onto the card base. Secure the model by fitting the prongs, located under its feet, into the holes in the base.

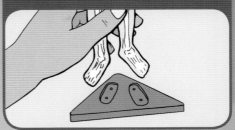

How to assemble your cardboard model

Take the two body shapes and slot them together. Make sure that each side matches (veins, arteries, and front and back muscles) so that you have a four-sided figure.

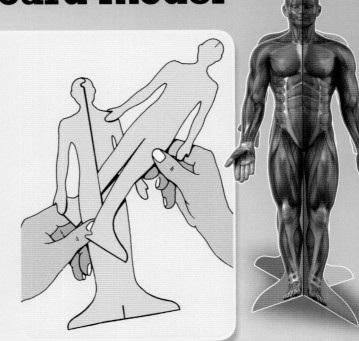

Body systems

Human bodies may look different from each other on the outside, but on the inside they all have the same body systems. These work together to keep you alive and healthy.

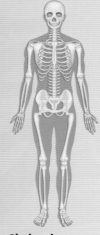

Skeletal system
Provides the body's inner framework.

Muscular system
Three different kinds of muscles help your body move.

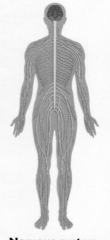

Nervous system
The body's control center.

Respiratory system
Supplies the body with essential oxygen.

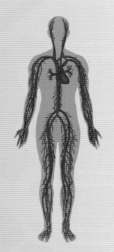

Circulatory system
Pumps blood, which carries oxygen and nutrients around the body.

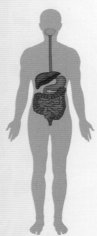

Digestive system
Turns the food you eat into energy.

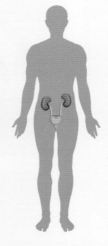

Urinary system
Removes waste products from your body.

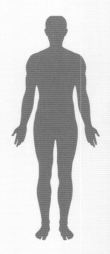

Skin
Your largest organ, which covers the body and protects the organs.

Building blocks

Your body is made up of more than 50 billion microscopic units called cells. Most cells contain structures called organelles, which means "little organs." At the center of each cell is the nucleus. This contains the genes that instruct the cell how to grow, work, and reproduce.

Cells combine to make tissues, tissues combine to make organs, and organs combine to make organisms—such as the human body!

Organ system

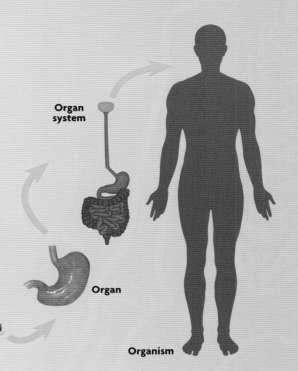

Organ

Cell

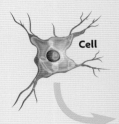

Tissue

Organism

Types of cells

Body cells come in different shapes and sizes, but an average human cell is about one thousandth of an inch wide. There are about 200 different types of human body cells. Some fight disease, some produce movement, and others store nutrients or make proteins. For instance, nerve cells carry electrical messages around the body; skin cells form a protective barrier around the body and hold it together; and new life begins when an egg and a sperm cell join together.

Nerve cell

Muscle cells

Skeletal (voluntary)

Smooth (involuntary)

Cardiac

Bone cell

Blood cells

Red blood cells

White blood cells

Platelets

Gland cells

Endocrine gland

Cells

Reproductive cells

Sperm

Egg

Skeleton

The skeleton is the body's inner framework. It is made up of more than 200 connected bones. Each bone performs a special job.

Long bones, such as those in the arms and legs, give the limbs strength and structure. Flatter bones, such as the ribs, protect organs.

Bones are strong yet supple. They meet at joints, which allow the bones to move against each other so that the body can move in a variety of ways.

Piece together your 15-part skeleton.

Skull

Breastbone (sternum)

Collarbone (clavicle)

Shoulder blade (scapula)

Ribs

Backbone (vertebrae)

Arm bones
humerus

ulna

radius

Hand bones
carpals

metacarpals

phalanges

Thighbone (femur)

Hip bone (pelvis)

Kneecap (patella)

Shin bones
tibia

fibula

Foot bones
tarsals
metatarsals
phalanges

Stapes
The smallest bone in the body, it sits inside the ear.

The ultimate biomaterial

Bone has the same strength as cast iron, but is still as light as wood. Because it is live tissue, any bone that suffers a fracture or break will quickly begin to heal.

Inside a bone

Our bones are filled with living material. There are blood vessels that run near the surface, then a layer called compact bone, and within that a spongier layer. Often there is a jellylike area in the center of the bone, which is the bone marrow. This produces all kinds of blood cells: red blood cells that carry oxygen, white blood cells that fight infections, and platelets that help blood to clot.

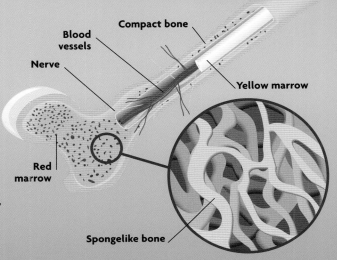

Compact bone

Blood vessels

Nerve

Yellow marrow

Red marrow

Spongelike bone

Types of bone joints

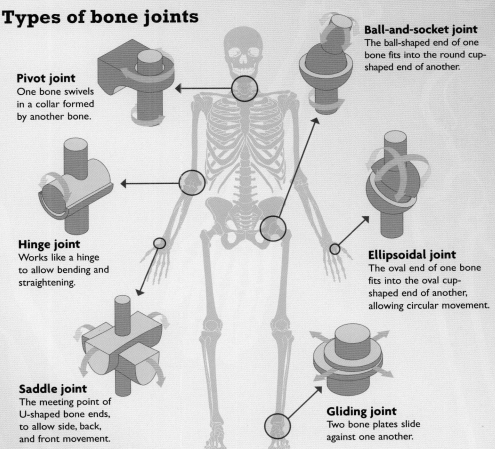

Pivot joint
One bone swivels in a collar formed by another bone.

Ball-and-socket joint
The ball-shaped end of one bone fits into the round cup-shaped end of another.

Hinge joint
Works like a hinge to allow bending and straightening.

Ellipsoidal joint
The oval end of one bone fits into the oval cup-shaped end of another, allowing circular movement.

Saddle joint
The meeting point of U-shaped bone ends, to allow side, back, and front movement.

Gliding joint
Two bone plates slide against one another.

Paper skeleton

Make your own skeleton model out of cardboard and learn how your bones all hang together.

You will need

- Thin white cardboard
- Tracing paper
- Pencil
- Scissors
- 14 paper fasteners
- String

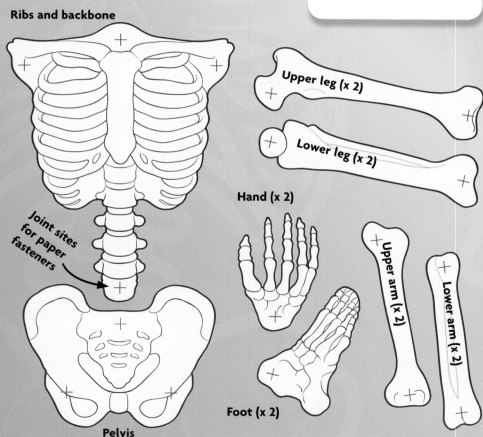

Skull

Ribs and backbone

Upper leg (x 2)

Lower leg (x 2)

Hand (x 2)

Upper arm (x 2)

Lower arm (x 2)

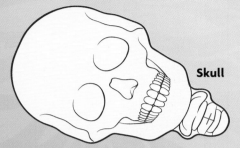

Joint sites for paper fasteners

Foot (x 2)

Pelvis

1 Trace or copy the bone shapes on the left onto your cardboard, including the red crosses. When you draw the second hand and foot, make sure you flip the image so that you have one left and one right of each.

2 Carefully cut out the shapes, and make small holes in the card where the red crosses are.

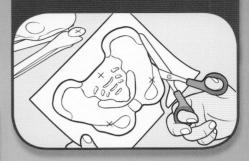

3 Link the pieces together at the joints using the paper fasteners. If you forget what goes where, turn back to page 6 to check!

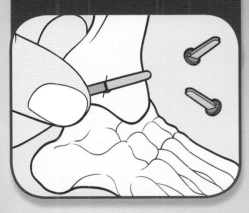

4 When you've finished assembling the skeleton, make a tiny hole at the top of the skull and thread a piece of string through it so that you can hang it up.

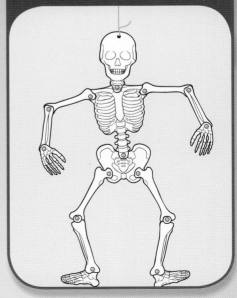

Design tip

Use glow-in-the-dark paper, or paint your bones with glow-in-the-dark paint, for a skeleton that is sure to give your friends a nighttime fright!

Muscular system

The body has three main types of muscle: skeletal, smooth, and cardiac muscle.

There are about 650 muscles in the body, and they make up about half your body weight. Skeletal muscles are those that work with your bones so that you can move, pick things up, or kick a ball. They are "voluntary muscles," which means that you decide when to use them and you control what they do.

Smooth and cardiac muscles work automatically. These are known as "involuntary muscles," and they are found in the heart, intestines, bladder, and other parts of the body. Your brain and body tell them what to do without your even thinking about it.

Slot together your circulatory and muscular system.

Muscles at the front of your body

Deltoid lifts the arm.

Pectoralis pulls the arm toward the body.

Biceps bends the arms.

Quadriceps femoris straightens the leg.

Muscle types

Skeletal muscles

Skeletal muscles enable you to move your body. They are held to your bones by strong cords called tendons. Together, the skeletal muscles work with your bones to give your body power and strength.

Smooth muscles

Smooth muscles line your digestive tract. They push food along the intestine. Smooth muscles in the bladder squeeze out urine. These involuntary muscles work slowly without ever getting tired.

Cardiac muscles

The cardiac muscle is an involuntary muscle that is found only in the heart. It contracts and relaxes throughout your life, pumping blood through your body.

Extensor digitorum longus straightens the toes and helps lift the foot upward.

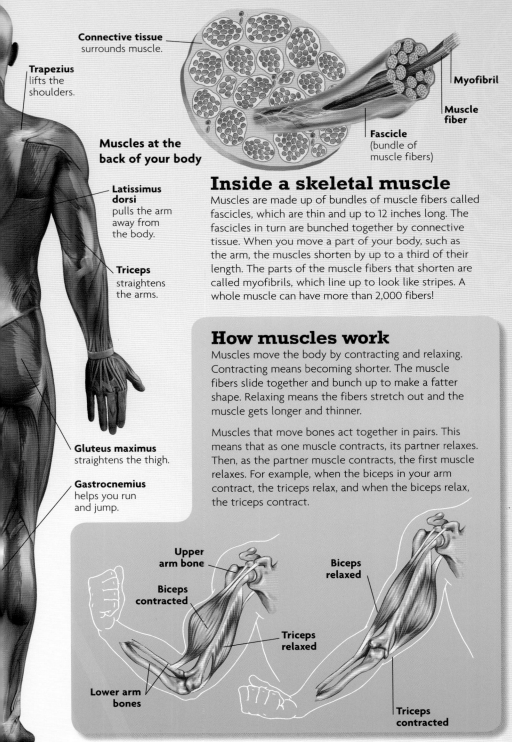

Connective tissue
surrounds muscle.

Trapezius
lifts the
shoulders.

**Muscles at the
back of your body**

**Latissimus
dorsi**
pulls the arm
away from
the body.

Triceps
straightens
the arms.

Gluteus maximus
straightens the thigh.

Gastrocnemius
helps you run
and jump.

Myofibril

**Muscle
fiber**

Fascicle
(bundle of
muscle fibers)

Inside a skeletal muscle

Muscles are made up of bundles of muscle fibers called fascicles, which are thin and up to 12 inches long. The fascicles in turn are bunched together by connective tissue. When you move a part of your body, such as the arm, the muscles shorten by up to a third of their length. The parts of the muscle fibers that shorten are called myofibrils, which line up to look like stripes. A whole muscle can have more than 2,000 fibers!

How muscles work

Muscles move the body by contracting and relaxing. Contracting means becoming shorter. The muscle fibers slide together and bunch up to make a fatter shape. Relaxing means the fibers stretch out and the muscle gets longer and thinner.

Muscles that move bones act together in pairs. This means that as one muscle contracts, its partner relaxes. Then, as the partner muscle contracts, the first muscle relaxes. For example, when the biceps in your arm contract, the triceps relax, and when the biceps relax, the triceps contract.

**Upper
arm bone**

**Biceps
contracted**

**Triceps
relaxed**

**Lower arm
bones**

**Biceps
relaxed**

**Triceps
contracted**

Make a working hand

Pull the stringy tendons to work the straw muscles, and this model hand will curl up its fingers like a real hand.

① Draw around your hand onto the piece of cardboard to create a hand shape. Carefully cut out the shape.

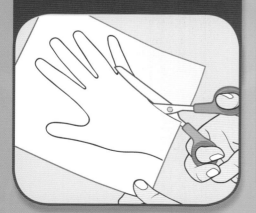

② Place a straw along one of the fingers with the end of the straw at the fingertip. Mark the position of the base of the finger on the straw. Then mark the positions of the other two finger joints.

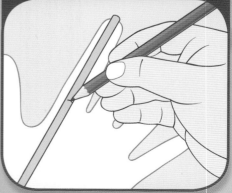

3

Snip out triangle shapes at the places where you've made the marks. Make sure these slits are on only one side of the straw.

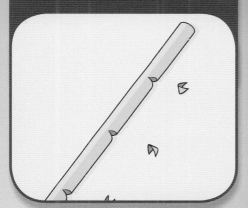

4

Repeat steps 2 and 3 for the other three fingers. Cut only two slits for the thumb (your thumb has only two joints). Then, with the slits facing upward, tape all the straws onto the fingertips and the palm.

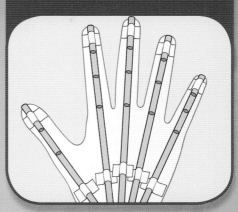

5

Cut five pieces of string about twice the length of the straws. Thread one through each straw and tape the end of the strings firmly to the cardboard fingertips.

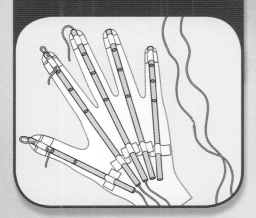

6

Now hold the hand at the wrist and gently pull the five strings toward you. See how the fingers bend at the joints to make your model hand move!

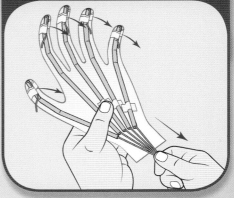

Nervous system

The human nervous system is the control center of the body. It is driven by the brain, which is about the size of a cantaloupe. Your brain is more complex than the world's most sophisticated computer.

Locate the brain in the model's skull.

The brain has three main regions: the brain stem, the cerebellum, and the cerebrum. The brain stem controls vital functions such as heartbeat, breathing, and blood pressure. The cerebellum helps to control your muscles and balance. The cerebrum is the brain's largest part, and is divided into two halves, or hemispheres. Aside from controlling your actions, the cerebrum receives and interprets all kinds of information from the outside world.

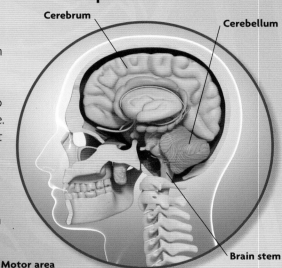

Cerebrum

Cerebellum

Brain stem

Motor area
The muscles that make your body move are controlled by the motor area.

Thinking area
The front part of your brain enables you to think, learn, plan, and feel.

Sensory area
The sensory area receives messages from the skin, nose, and tongue.

Left hemisphere

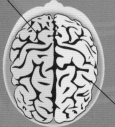

Right hemisphere

Sight area
The back of the cerebrum is the area used to see. It interprets the messages sent from your eyes.

Left or right?

Each hemisphere controls its own unique set of activities, or tasks. The right side of the brain tends to be more dominant in creative activities, while the left side of the brain tends to take charge of more logical or analytical activities, like math.

Hearing area
The hearing area receives messages from the ears.

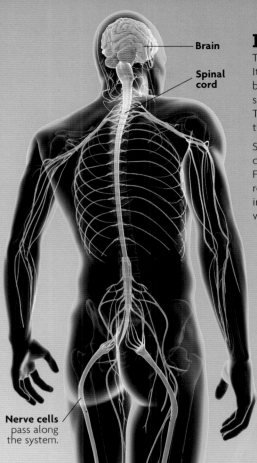

Brain

Spinal cord

Nerve cells pass along the system.

How it works

The brain is at the top of the nervous system. It sends messages to the various parts of the body by nerve cells, which pass down the spinal cord and travel to the rest of the body. The spinal cord runs through the middle of the backbone.

Some of the nervous system is under your control, but a lot of it works automatically. For example, these nonvoluntary actions, or reflexes, make you sneeze when your nose is irritated, sweat when you are hot, and shiver when you are cold.

Spinal cord

The spinal cord is a bundle of nerve fibers that runs through the backbone. Signals travel back and forth through the fibers to the body. Sensory neurons in the nervous system bring messages to the spinal cord, and motor neurons deliver messages to the muscles.

Hormonal system

The hormonal system is a set of glands called endocrine glands that release chemicals, called hormones, into the blood. Hormones travel throughout the body and tell specific cells what to do. The body has seven main hormonal glands.

Adrenal glands make hormones such as adrenaline, which prepares your body to react quickly in stressful situations.

Pancreas makes hormones such as insulin, which controls blood sugar levels.

Pineal gland controls sleep patterns.

Pituitary gland releases hormones that control growth.

Thyroid gland produces a hormone that controls the speed of chemical reactions in body cells.

Thymus gland helps children fight diseases.

Ovaries (female) or testes (male) are reproductive organs. They produce hormones that affect bodily development and reproduction.

15

Test your reactions

It is difficult to measure reaction times because your brain and body work so fast. The first experiment uses the markings on a ruler to record the speed of your reactions.

You will need

- 12-inch ruler
- Notebook
- A window
- Cotton balls

1
Ask a friend to hold the ruler upright, with the 12-inch mark at the top. Hold your thumb and finger apart, level with the bottom of the ruler.

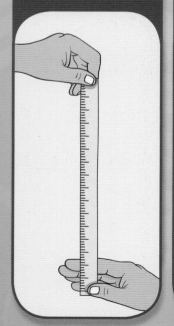

2
Your friend then has to let go of the ruler. You have to catch it as soon as you see it start to fall.

3

RESULTS

Person	Distance
Me	6 inches
Raj	4 inches
Tyrone	7 inches
Robyn	8 inches
Mom	5 inches

The measurement at which your thumb grabs the ruler is your score. The lower the number, the faster your nervous system is working! Ask friends and family to try it, too, to see how much the results vary.

Try the same test, but use your other hand. Is the number any lower?

Knee jerk!

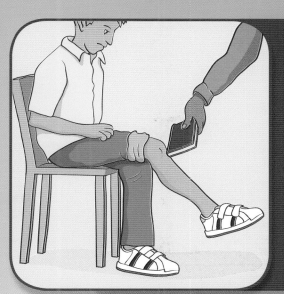

Sit on a chair with one leg crossed over the other. Ask someone to tap your upper knee sharply, just below the kneecap, with the edge of the notebook.

Your knee kicks when it's tapped. The spinal cord controls this reflex. It's part of the "proprioception" system that helps your balance.

Don't blink!

Stand behind a window or clear glass door, with your face up against the glass. Ask someone to throw cotton balls at your face *from the other side of the glass.* Your challenge is to keep your eyes open. Can you do it?

Even though you know you're behind glass, your body has a reflex that shuts your eyes, so it's very difficult not to blink. This reflex protects your eyes when something flies toward them.

Respiratory system

Breathing supplies the body with oxygen, which is essential for converting food into energy. The other function of the respiratory system is to get rid of carbon dioxide—the waste product of energy production.

The respiratory system is made up of two lungs and the channel along which the air passes into and out of them. The channel begins at the nose and mouth and travels down the throat and into the lungs. When you breathe through your nose, air enters and becomes warm and moist. Sticky mucus and hairs inside the nose trap dirt, dust, and any tiny particles before the air travels to the lungs.

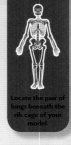

Locate the pair of lungs beneath the rib cage of your model.

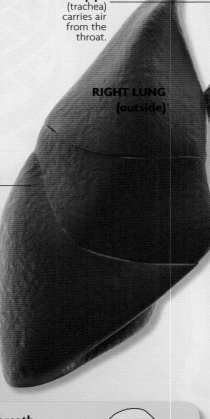

Windpipe
(trachea) carries air from the throat.

RIGHT LUNG
(outside)

Lungs
are made of spongy tissue.

How do we breathe?

Many parts of your body work together to take air into the lungs and expel carbon dioxide.

Lungs do not contain any muscle fibers and cannot expand on their own. It is the movements of the muscles surrounding the ribs as well as a large muscle called the diaphragm that make the lungs expand and contract (see the balloon lung experiment on page 20).

In breath

When you breathe in, the diaphragm muscles flatten out and push downward. At the same time, the muscles between the ribs contract and pull the ribs upward and outward. This enlarges the chest area, allowing the lungs to fill up with air.

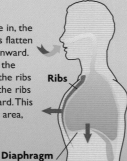

Ribs

Diaphragm

Out breath

When you breathe out, your diaphragm moves upward and your ribs move downward and inward. The chest is now smaller; the lungs shrink back in size and force the air out.

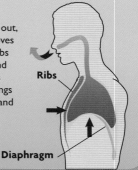

Ribs

Diaphragm

The diaphragm's other roles

Sneezing is a sudden release of built-up air pressure.

Hiccuping happens when the diaphragm is irritated.

The sound of **laughter** is caused by contractions of the diaphragm.

Coughing is a blast of air that clears particles from the windpipe.

Bronchus takes air into each lung.

Exchanging gases

Inside the chest, the windpipe divides into two branches, or bronchi—one for each lung. The bronchi divide thousands of times into increasingly narrow tubes called bronchioles, which can be less than 1 millimeter in diameter. At the end of these fine bronchioles are balloon-like sacs shaped like a bunch of grapes. These are called alveoli, and they are smaller than a grain of salt. They have thin, moist walls that gas can pass through easily. There are more than 300 million alveoli in each lung. If they were flattened out, they could cover an area as big as a tennis court!

LEFT LUNG (inside)

Bronchiole takes air into sacs (alveoli) where oxygen is swapped for carbon dioxide.

Bronchiole

Alveoli

Blood capillary

Activity

When you are resting you breathe in and out 10 to 14 times a minute. Try running in place for a minute. You will find that your breathing becomes much faster—up to 30 times a minute.

19

Balloon lung

This experiment shows how your diaphragm helps to open up your lungs and suck in air.

1

Dangle one of the balloons inside the bottle. Stretch the balloon opening over the neck of the bottle. Cut off the bottom of the bottle with scissors.

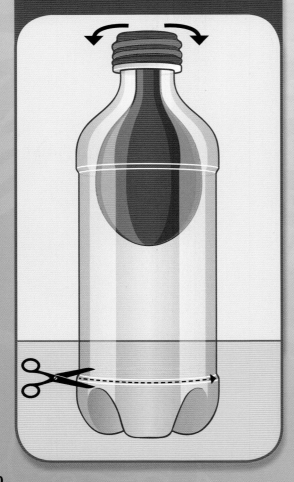

2

Cut the neck off the other balloon and stretch the rest over the bottom of the bottle. Secure it in place with the rubber band.

DEEPEST BREATH

The longest time someone has held their breath was more than 20 minutes, but that's not normal! Most of us can manage only a minute or two. You have to keep breathing or your cells will start to run out of oxygen.

3

Now hold the bottle in one hand. With the other hand, pinch the lower balloon in the middle and gently pull it downward. Watch what happens to the balloon at the top.

◀ Free divers swim as deep as they can while holding their breath. Record-holding free divers can hold their breath 11 minutes or more!

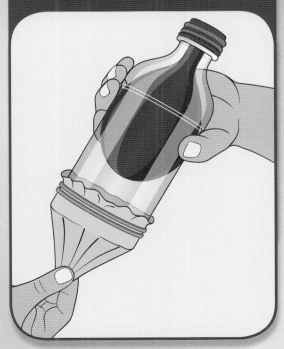

What's happening?

The balloon at the top is the model lung, and the balloon at the bottom is the diaphragm. As the diaphragm pulls down, it increases volume and reduces pressure inside the bottle. This sucks air into the balloon lung.

Inside the heart

Your heart is a reliable pump. When you are resting it beats about 70 times a minute. It pumps about 100,000 times a day—or 40 million times a year!

Locate the heart in your model.

Your heart is the size of a fist and is like a two-story house with four rooms. Each room is called a chamber. The right and left atria are the upper chambers. The right and left ventricles are the lower chambers. The right atrium receives the blood that is low in oxygen and pumps it into the right ventricle. The right ventricle then pumps the blood through the pulmonary artery to the lungs to receive oxygen. Newly oxygenated blood is sent back from the lungs to the heart, this time to the left atrium, where it is then pumped into the left ventricle. The oxygen-rich blood is then pumped out through the aorta to the entire body.

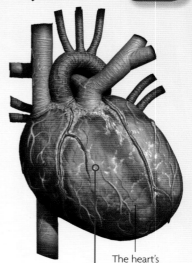

The heart's walls are made of strong muscle called **myocardium**.

Heart valves

The heart also has valves that open and close at the right time to control the direction of blood flow. Blood passes through this one-way valve into the ventricle, which forces blood out into the pulmonary arteries, from where it flows to the lungs to receive oxygen.

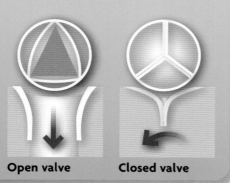

Open valve   **Closed valve**

Muscle cells contract to push blood through the blood vessels.

The body's pump

The heart pumps blood around the body to supply oxygen wherever it is needed, and once the oxygen is used up, the blood is pumped back to the lungs to pick up its next load of oxygen.

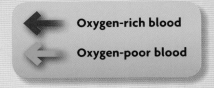

Oxygen-rich blood

Oxygen-poor blood

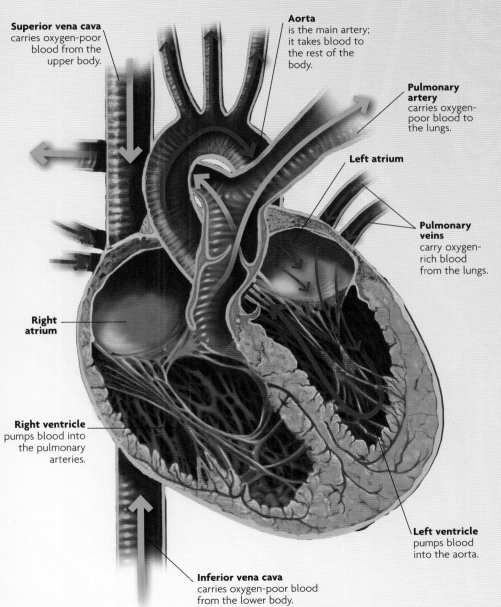

Superior vena cava
carries oxygen-poor blood from the upper body.

Aorta
is the main artery; it takes blood to the rest of the body.

Pulmonary artery
carries oxygen-poor blood to the lungs.

Left atrium

Pulmonary veins
carry oxygen-rich blood from the lungs.

Right atrium

Right ventricle
pumps blood into the pulmonary arteries.

Left ventricle
pumps blood into the aorta.

Inferior vena cava
carries oxygen-poor blood from the lower body.

23

Paper valves

This simple model shows you how a heart valve works. It even makes a "lub-dub" beating noise, much like a real heart.

You will need

- Paper cup or yogurt pot
- Scissors
- 1-inch-square piece of paper
- Tape

1

Cut a hole about half an inch across in the base of the cup.

2

Place the cup tightly over your mouth and breathe in and out through it. Air passes through the hole in both directions.

3

Now cut out a square of paper about an inch across. Put it over the hole at the bottom, and tape it in place along one edge.

4

Bring the cup to your mouth like before and breathe in and out. Air now passes through the hole in only one direction: outward. The paper valve prevents air from coming in.

What's happening?

You have made a working valve. When air goes through it one way, it pushes the valve open. Air coming back the other way makes the valve flap shut. You can breathe out through the hole, but the valve keeps you from breathing in.

Stethoscope

Doctors use stethoscopes to hear the sounds of the heart more clearly. Use this working model to listen to your friends' heartbeats.

You will need

- Cardboard tube from a roll of paper towels or toilet paper
- Small funnel
- Tape

1 Fit the funnel inside one end of the tube.

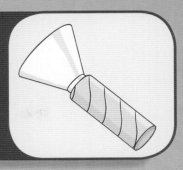

2 Hold the funnel in place and wrap the tape around to join.

3 Place the funnel against a friend's chest. Put your ear to the other end of the tube. Can you hear his or her heartbeat clearly?

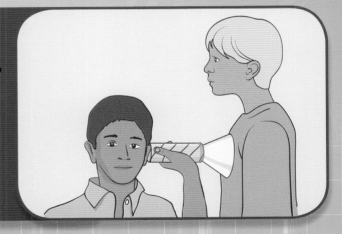

Circulatory system

There are about five liters of blood in an adult body. Your heart pumps it through a system of arteries that carry it to every part of the body.

These arteries branch many times and become increasingly narrow until they are tiny capillaries. Capillaries have walls just one cell thick. Chemicals from digested food that are carried in the blood pass through these walls into the body cells to keep them alive and well nourished.

Slot together your circulatory and muscular systems.

Jugular veins return oxygen-poor blood from the brain to the heart's right side.

Carotid artery takes oxygen-rich blood to the brain.

Aorta is the largest artery.

Radial artery leads to the front forearm.

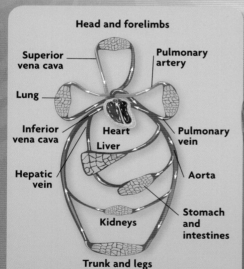

Head and forelimbs

Superior vena cava

Pulmonary artery

Lung

Inferior vena cava

Heart

Liver

Pulmonary vein

Hepatic vein

Aorta

Kidneys

Stomach and intestines

Trunk and legs

How blood circulates

Blood travels along the body through a network of specialized vessels. Most major body parts have an artery and vein. The artery (red) brings blood fresh in nutrients and oxygen into the body, and the vein (blue) takes away waste. Blood circulation is driven by the heart.

Femoral vein returns oxygen-poor blood from the legs to the right side of the heart.

Inferior vena cava returns oxygen-poor blood from the lower body to the right side of the heart.

Dorsal digital vein returns oxygen-poor blood from the toes back to the heart.

Femoral artery supplies oxygen-rich blood to the legs.

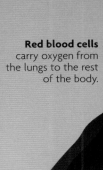

Red blood cells
carry oxygen from
the lungs to the rest
of the body.

Arteries and veins

Arteries carry blood away from the heart. Arteries have
th ck, stretchy walls that help them to cope with high-pressure
blood flow. Veins have thin, floppy walls carrying blood at a
lower pressure, as well as valves that prevent backflow.

Blood cells

Under a microscope, the three main kinds
of blood cells are visible. Red cells carry
oxygen, and are by far the most numerous.
White cells attack germs and clean the
blood. Platelets help blood to clot, making it
thick and sticky to seal a cut. All these cells
float in plasma, the liquid part of blood.

Plasma
is made mainly of water, but
there are a large number of
substances dissolved in it, such
as sugar, fats, hormones, and
waste products like carbon
dioxide and urea.

White blood cells
are produced in bone
marrow. Their main
purpose is to fight
germs and infections
in the body.

Platelets
are also formed in the
bone marrow. They help
stop bleeding from a cut
by forming a clot.

Measure your pulse

You can feel your heartbeat all around your body. Each pump of the heart makes blood surge, or pulse, through the blood vessels. Here's how to feel your pulse and "see" it in action!

Take your pulse

1 Hold one hand with your palm facing upward. Now place the first two fingers of your other hand on your wrist, on the same side as your thumb, just below the crease between the wrist and the hand.

2 When you find the right place, you should feel the pulse as a little bumping sensation under your fingertips. To measure your pulse, use a clock or a stopwatch to count how many beats there are in one minute. This is your pulse rate.

3 Try measuring your pulse rate when you're relaxed, then again after having done some exercise, such as running in place for a minute. Is there much difference?

Pulse twitcher

- **Marshmallow**
- **Toothpick**

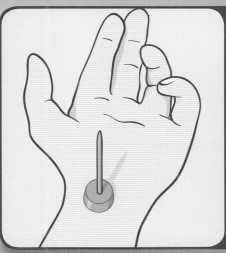

Stick the toothpick halfway into the marshmallow. Press the marshmallow onto your pulse point with the stick pointing upward. Once you get the placing just right, your pulse should make the stick twitch back and forth. Now you can see your pulse!

Exercise such as swimming makes your heart beat faster. This causes the blood to flow faster, so it can deliver more oxygen, and your cells can work harder. Being scared can make your heart race, too. Your body is preparing in case you have to run away!

An average adult's pulse rate when at rest is about 70 beats per minute. Children's hearts usually beat a little faster than this.

Upper digestive system

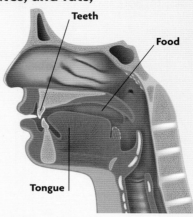
You have to eat food to live. Food is made of many different substances. You need some of these, such as protein, carbohydrates, and fats, to grow and stay healthy.

Before it can nourish your body, food has to be broken down into small and simple pieces. The body can then absorb these tiny pieces into the bloodstream and make the nutrients available to the cells. This process is called digestion. The digestive system takes the form of a tube about 30 feet long, which is fitted with a number of organs. Each organ along this tube has a special part to play. Your food starts its long journey at the mouth.

Teeth

Food

Tongue

1. You chew food with your teeth to break it down. The tongue presses this food against the palate (roof of the mouth) and mixes it with saliva to mash it further and create a ball of food called a "bolus."

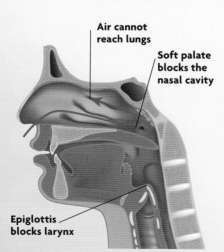

Air cannot reach lungs

Soft palate blocks the nasal cavity

Epiglottis blocks larynx

2. When you are ready to swallow the bolus, the throat muscles squeeze food down the esophagus. At the same time, the lidlike epiglottis closes the entrance to the windpipe (trachea). This prevents food from going down into the lungs.

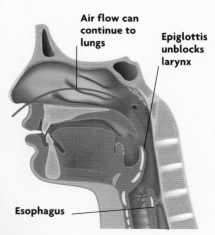

Air flow can continue to lungs

Epiglottis unblocks larynx

Esophagus

3. Once you've swallowed the food, the epiglottis opens up again so you can continue to breathe. Meanwhile, the food travels down the esophagus and enters the second stage of digestion.

Your stomach

It takes about seven seconds for food to reach the stomach. A ring of muscles at the bottom of the esophagus relaxes to allow food into the stomach. By squeezing and relaxing, your stomach crushes food into a pulp while mixing it with acidic digestive juices produced by glands in the stomach lining. Then, food passes into the first part of the small intestine, called the duodenum, which continues the digestion process. This tube folds back and forth, giving it a much larger area for absorbing food.

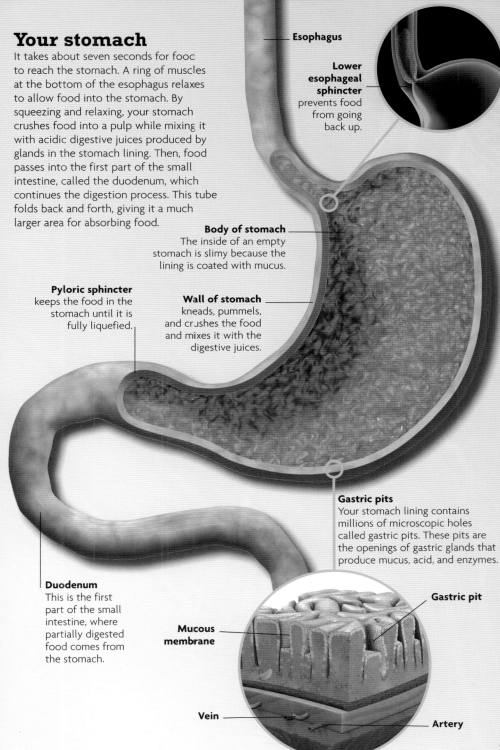

Esophagus

Lower esophageal sphincter
prevents food from going back up.

Body of stomach
The inside of an empty stomach is slimy because the lining is coated with mucus.

Pyloric sphincter
keeps the food in the stomach until it is fully liquefied.

Wall of stomach
kneads, pummels, and crushes the food and mixes it with the digestive juices.

Gastric pits
Your stomach lining contains millions of microscopic holes called gastric pits. These pits are the openings of gastric glands that produce mucus, acid, and enzymes.

Gastric pit

Mucous membrane

Duodenum
This is the first part of the small intestine, where partially digested food comes from the stomach.

Vein

Artery

Model stomach

You will need

- Two small plastic bags with zipper closures
- Vinegar
- Small beaker or cup
- Graham crackers or other hard, dry crackers (not crumbly ones)
- Water

Your stomach is basically a bag full of acid that breaks down the food that passes through it. You can use household items to make your own model stomach.

2 Break a cracker into small pieces as if you have chewed it. Put the pieces into the bag with the water and seal the bag. Now break up a second cracker. Put the pieces into the bag with the vinegar and seal this bag, too.

1 Put a small cupful of water into one bag. Put the same amount of vinegar into the second bag.

3

Leave the two bags for a few minutes for the liquid to soak in. Then pick up each bag in turn, and squash it to represent the action of the stomach muscles. Which bag is better at dissolving the cracker?

4

Now try this with one broken cracker and one whole cracker in each bag. This will show you if chewing food before you swallow helps the stomach to dissolve it faster. Try out other food, such as hard and soft candies, a banana, cheese, or cereal.

What's happening?
Like the liquid in your stomach, vinegar is an acid. It is good at dissolving food and breaking it down. The cracker in the vinegar dissolves more quickly than the one in the water because water is not acidic, and dissolves things more slowly.

Why doesn't your stomach digest itself?
The acid in your stomach can break down all kinds of food, including meat, which is made of muscle just like the stomach. But the stomach itself isn't dissolved. That's because its lining releases a thick, slimy mucus that coats it all over, protecting it from the acid.

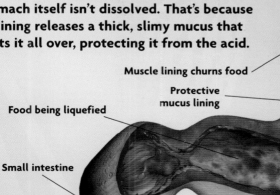

Muscle lining churns food

Protective mucus lining

Food being liquefied

Small intestine

Lower digestive system

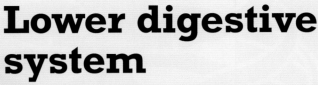

Locate the intestines in your model.

At more than 19 feet long, the small intestine is the longest part of the digestive tract.

Inside the small intestine, digestive juices from the stomach, gallbladder, and pancreas continue to break food into minuscule particles. These are then absorbed by tiny blood vessels. Some of the particles are taken to the liver for more processing, and the rest are carried to the areas of the body where they are used.

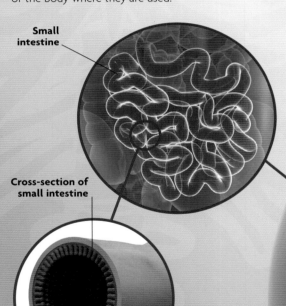

Small intestine

Cross-section of small intestine

Villi

Villi
The lining of the small intestine is full of folds and ridges that are covered in millions of tiny "fingers" called villi. The food that enters the small intestine has been reduced to tiny particles, and they pass through these villi into the bloodstream to feed the body.

Liver

The liver is the largest single organ inside your body. It lies in the top right-hand part of the abdomen. The liver is like a chemical processing factory, a food storage system, and blood cleaner rolled into one. It receives the digested food through the blood vessels and processes them to make simple chemicals like glucose, which it stores and then releases back into the bloodstream when the body needs it. The liver also removes poisons, such as alcohol, from the blood.

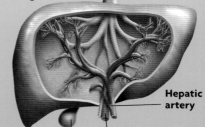

Hepatic portal vein brings in blood from the digestive tract.

Hepatic artery

Gallbladder secretes enzymes that flow into the duodenum and help digestion.

Bile from the bile duct flows into the duodenum and helps to digest fats.

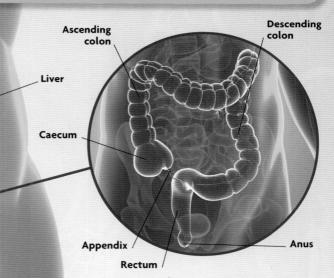

Ascending colon

Descending colon

Liver

Caecum

Appendix

Rectum

Anus

Large intestine

After the nutrients from food have been absorbed through the small intestine, the undigested matter passes into the large intestine. This is another tube about 5 feet long and 3 inches wide, and ends at a muscular ring called the anus. The job of the large intestine is to absorb water from the undigested food, which then becomes a semisolid waste called feces, or poop. Feces is stored in the last part of the large intestine, called the rectum, and is pushed out through the anus when you go to the bathroom.

Measure your guts

As you know, the food that you eat goes on a long, winding journey through your body. If you could unwind your digestive system and lay it out, it would reach halfway across a soccer field! To find out how long yours is, try this stringy activity.

You will need

- Large ball of string
- Tape measure
- Calculator
- Scissors
- Sticker labels
- Pen
- A large floor area

1
Make a fist and measure how wide it is. Multiply by 2 to find the length of your mouth and throat. Cut a piece of string this long. Stick a label around the string and write "mouth and throat" on the label.

2
Your esophagus is about the length of your hand span—the distance from your thumb to your little finger when you stretch out your hand. Cut a piece of string this long and label it "esophagus."

3 Just before you eat, your stomach is about the size and width of one fist. Cut a piece of string this long and label it "stomach."

4 The length of your small intestine is just over 3 times your full height. Measure how tall you are. Multiply this by 3.5 and cut a piece of string that long. Label it "small intestine."

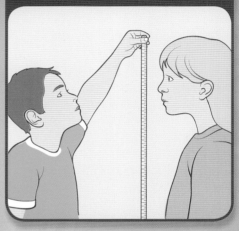

5 Your large intestine is about a quarter of the length of your small intestine. Divide the length of your small intestine by 4 and cut a piece of string this long. Label it "large intestine."

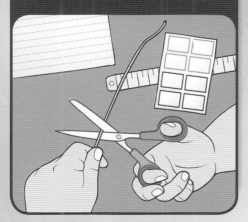

6 Finally, take your pieces of string and lay them out end-to-end in a long, straight line on the floor and measure the length. This is how long your whole digestive system is!

Skin and hair

Your whole body is covered in a flexible layer of skin. The skin is the largest organ of the body.

The skin has several jobs: it protects you from minor bumps and scrapes. It also prevents germs, chemicals, and sunlight from causing damage to deeper tissues. Because it is waterproof, skin stops water from getting into the body, and fluids from leaking out. A brown or black color in the skin, called melanin, helps prevent harmful ultraviolet rays in sunlight from damaging the body. The lighter the skin, the less melanin it produces, which is why fair-skinned people have to be more careful of the sun.

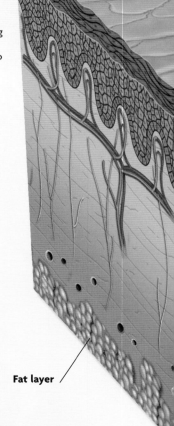

The skin is the body's largest organ.

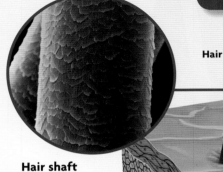

Hair

Hair shaft
Your body is covered in millions of hairs. They spring from cells found at the bottom of deep holes in the skin.

Hot and cold

When your body is hot, you begin to sweat. As the sweat evaporates from the surface of your skin, heat is lost and your body cools down. The little hairs on your skin play a part in keeping you warm, a trait left over from the time before humans regularly wore clothes. When you are cold, the hair erector muscles contract, producing "goose bumps," which cause the hairs to stand up. Warm air is trapped between the hairs and acts as a layer of insulation.

Sweat
Sweat drops appear on the surface of the skin when the moisture leaves through tiny holes known as pores.

Goose bumps
Whenever you are cold or feel strong emotions like fear, the hair erector muscle under the skin makes the hairs stand up.

Fat layer

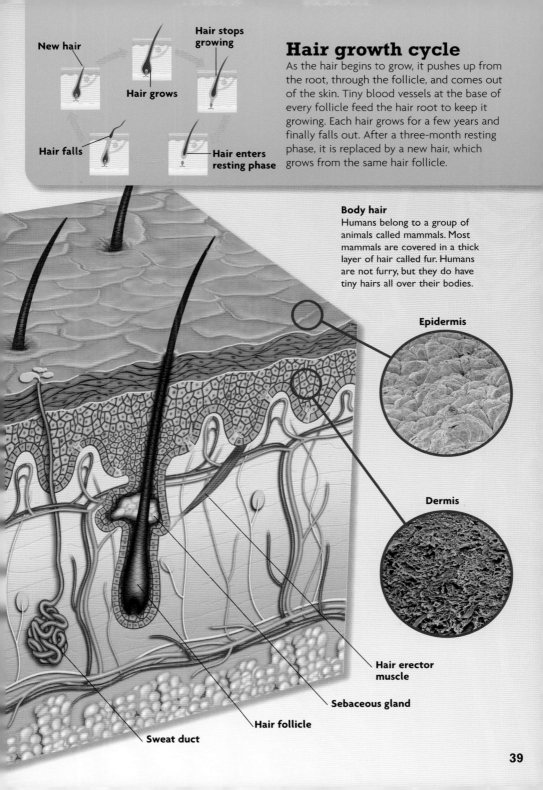

Hair growth cycle

New hair

Hair stops growing

Hair grows

Hair falls

Hair enters resting phase

As the hair begins to grow, it pushes up from the root, through the follicle, and comes out of the skin. Tiny blood vessels at the base of every follicle feed the hair root to keep it growing. Each hair grows for a few years and finally falls out. After a three-month resting phase, it is replaced by a new hair, which grows from the same hair follicle.

Body hair
Humans belong to a group of animals called mammals. Most mammals are covered in a thick layer of hair called fur. Humans are not furry, but they do have tiny hairs all over their bodies.

Epidermis

Dermis

Hair erector muscle

Sebaceous gland

Hair follicle

Sweat duct

Test your sense of touch

The skin has receptors that help people identify objects by touch. These receptors are more concentrated in some areas, such as the fingertips, than in others. Test how sensitive to touch your fingertips are.

You will need

- 6 pieces of sandpaper, each one a different grade
- Scissors
- Sticker labels

1

Find small samples—about 3 inches square—of sandpaper in six different grades, from superfine to very rough. The grades are usually printed on the back of the paper.

3

Now turn away and ask a friend to switch the pieces into a random order. Turn back with your eyes closed and try to reorder the pieces correctly using only your fingertips as a guide. When you're done, look to see how accurately you graded the papers. Swap roles to see if your friend can reorder the pieces.

2

Trim the pieces so they are all the same size and shape. Attach a sticker label to each piece, and number the labels in order of the sandpaper's roughness, from 1 to 6. Lay them in order—smoothest to roughest—in front of you. Close your eyes and touch each in turn.

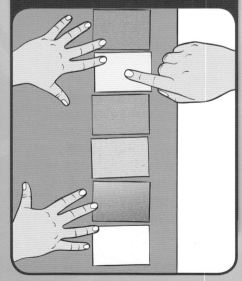

Sensitive areas

Aside from your fingertips, other parts of your body that are especially sensitive to touch include the cheeks, upper lip, palms, forehead, and feet. Compare the sensitivity of different parts of your body.

You will need

- Two metal paper clips
- Notepad and pencil

1

Unbend one metal paper clip to form a "U" shape, and a second one so it is straight.

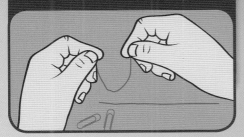

2

Make a list of different parts of the body and ask a friend to touch each of them in turn with (a) the single point of the straight wire or (b) the two prongs of the bent clip. Close your eyes so you don't know whether you are being touched with one point or with two, and ask your friend to record how many points you feel in each area.

3

Check the chart to see which are the more sensitive areas. Now swap roles and see if your friend scores differently.

Part of body	One point	Two points
Cheek		
Knee		
Forearm		
Shoulder		
Chin		
Foot		
Lip		
Back		
Calf		

What's happening?

The areas where you feel a single point when you were touched with two, such as the leg, have fewer touch receptors, which is why you can't feel both points.

41

Urinary system

Your body uses energy-rich nutrients to grow, stay alive, and repair itself. In doing so, it also makes waste products in the body cells, including carbon dioxide and salt. The body must get rid of this chemical waste, and it does so by a process called excretion.

Carbon dioxide and some water are excreted through the lungs, salt and more water are excreted through sweat, but most excretion takes place through the kidneys. They sit just above the waist, on either side of the spine, behind the stomach. They filter chemicals out of the bloodstream to produce urine. Your blood passes through the kidneys 300 times a day, producing about 1½ liters of urine.

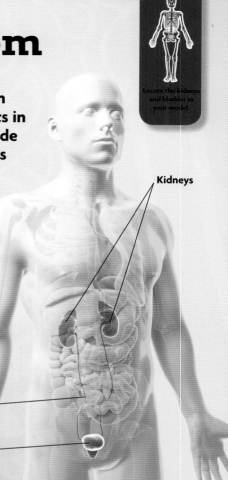

Locate the kidneys and bladder in your model.

Kidneys

Ureter
Urine trickles down this narrow pipe into the bladder.

Bladder
As the bladder fills with urine, it expands. When it is about 3 inches across, you feel the need to empty it.

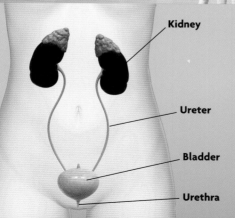

Kidney

Ureter

Bladder

Urethra

Kidneys

The kidneys are two reddish organs that look like beans and are your body's blood-cleaning factory. They contain microscopic filtering units that are working all the time to remove waste, unwanted minerals, and surplus water from the blood to make urine. Each kidney is connected to the bladder by a long tube called a ureter, through which urine trickles down to reach the bladder.

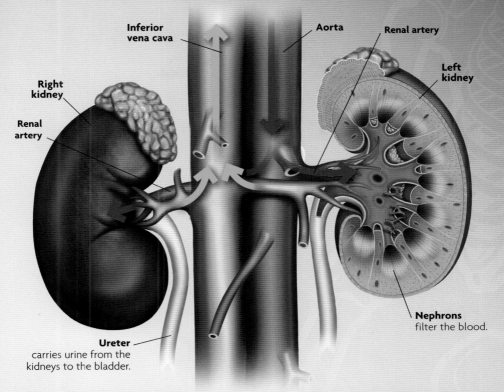

Inferior vena cava

Aorta

Renal artery

Left kidney

Right kidney

Renal artery

Nephrons
filter the blood.

Ureter
carries urine from the
kidneys to the bladder.

How does it work?

The blood carrying waste substances enters the kidneys
through the renal artery, which branches off the aorta (red
channel). Then microscopic filtration units called nephrons
inside the kidneys filter the blood to remove the waste and
make urine. At the same time, the clean blood leaves each
kidney and empties into the inferior vena cava (blue channel),
and returns to the heart.

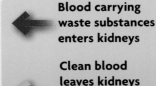

**Blood carrying
waste substances
enters kidneys**

**Clean blood
leaves kidneys
and returns to
heart**

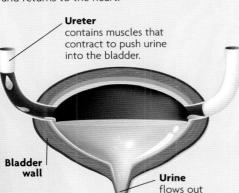

Ureter
contains muscles that
contract to push urine
into the bladder.

**Bladder
wall**

Urine
flows out
through the
urethra.

Bladder

The bladder is an elastic, muscular bag
made of layers of smooth muscle cells. It
can hold up to half a liter of urine. When it
is empty, the bladder lining contains many
folds; these smooth out and the muscle wall
thins as the bladder fills with urine from the
two ureters. From the bladder, urine passes
out of your body through a tube called the
urethra. The urethra is controlled by a strong
ring of muscle called a sphincter.

Keep yourself hydrated

Keep a hydration diary for a week and discover how much water you need to drink to make your body run efficiently.

Urine color chart

This color suggests adequate hydration.

An extra glass of water would be a good idea.

Your body needs more water in order to function efficiently.

You should drink water right away, and probably increase your daily intake.

Urine this color signals severe dehydration, which is dangerous and requires medical attention.

You will need

- **Weighing scales**
- **Measuring cup**
- **Notebook**

1

At the start of the week, notice the color of your urine and decide which of the shades on the chart it matches most closely. This will give you a good idea of your current hydration levels.

2

A human body needs about 8 ounces of water for every 10 pounds of its weight. To calculate how much you need to take in each day, weigh yourself, and then divide the number of pounds by 10. For example, if you weigh 80 pounds, you need to consume about eight 8-ounce cups of water a day.

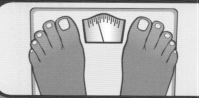

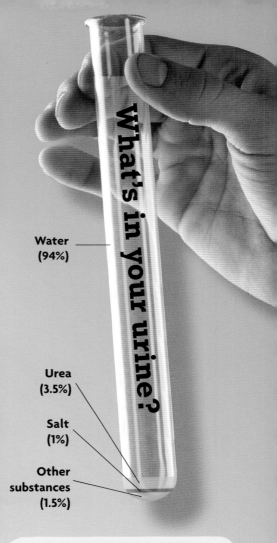

What's in your urine?

Water
(94%)

Urea
(3.5%)

Salt
(1%)

Other
substances
(1.5%)

3

Your body absorbs about half of the amount of water you need from your food (a banana is 75 percent water, for example). You make up the rest by drinking. So at 80 pounds of body weight, you will need to drink four 8-ounce glasses every day.

Use a measuring cup and pour 8 ounces of water into your favorite cup to find out what it looks like.

4

Each day for a week, record in your hydration diary just how much water you drink. At the end of the week, check your urine against the color chart once more. Has your hydration improved?

Why should I drink water?

If there's not enough water in your body, your intestines and kidneys work less efficiently, and your energy levels—among other things—will begin to flag. So help your body stay in tip-top condition by making sure it always has enough water.

Growing up

The body experiences many physical changes on its journey from birth to old age.

At birth, a person weighs 7–9 pounds and is about 19 inches tall. Over time he or she grows into an adult, becoming 15–20 times heavier and more than three times taller. At about 20 years of age, the body reaches its full adult size.

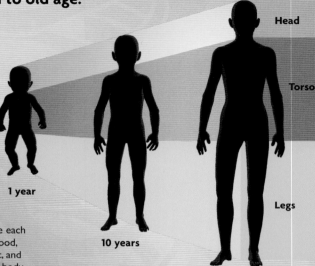

Head

Torso

Legs

1 year

10 years

20 years

Changing proportions
A newborn baby's head and legs are each one-quarter of its height. By adulthood, the head is one-eighth of the height, and the legs make up almost half of the body.

Skull development

A newborn baby's skull has soft gaps between the bones, called fontanels. These allow the skull to be squeezed slightly at birth so that the baby can pass through the mother's uterus and out of the birth canal. As the infant grows, the skull bones gradually enlarge and the gaps shrink. The adult skull has no gaps and the bones are fused along faint wavy lines, known as sutures.

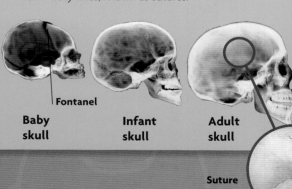

Fontanel

Baby skull

Infant skull

Adult skull

Suture

Aging hand

Hand X-rays highlight the difference between young and older bones. A child's skeleton may seem small because they are still partly made of a tough, elastic tissue called cartilage, which mostly develops into bone by adulthood. In old age, bones may become misshapen because of a disease called arthritis, which causes swelling and pain in the joints.

At age 2
An X-ray of a child's hand, showing cartilage growth plates that will turn into bone.

Cartilage growth plates

Stages of life

Babies grow quickly during their first year. Growth slows down during childhood, but speeds up again during puberty (the teenage years), when changes happen that make reproduction possible. By the age of 20, growth stops, and by the age of 30, the body starts to age gradually.

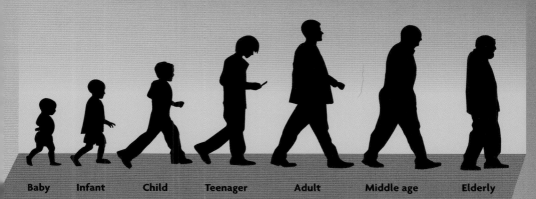

Baby   **Infant**   **Child**   **Teenager**   **Adult**   **Middle age**   **Elderly**

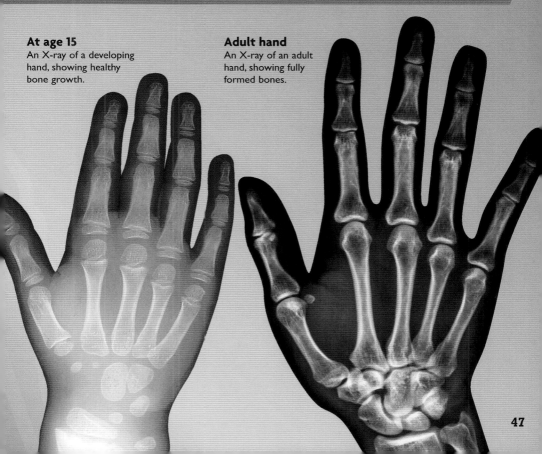

At age 15
An X-ray of a developing hand, showing healthy bone growth.

Adult hand
An X-ray of an adult hand, showing fully formed bones.

Index